Water Bugs

by Helen Frost

water boatman

Consulting Editor: Gail Saunders-Smith, Ph.D.

Consultant: Gary A. Dunn, Director of Education,
Young Entomologists' Society

Pebble Books

an imprint of Capstone Press
Mankato, Minnesota

Pebble Books are published by Capstone Press
151 Good Counsel Drive, P.O. Box 669, Mankato, Minnesota 56002
http://www.capstone-press.com

1 2 3 4 5 6 06 05 04 03 02 01

Library of Congress Cataloging-in-Publication Data
Frost, Helen, 1949–
     Water bugs/by Helen Frost.
     p. cm.—(Insects)
     Includes bibliographical references (p. 23) and index.
     ISBN 0-7368-0856-6
     1. Aquatic insects—Juvenile literature. 2. Belostomatidae—Juvenile
literature. [1. Water bugs.] I. Title. II. Insects (Mankato, Minn.)
QL472 .F76 2001
595.716—dc21   00-009674

Summary: Simple text and photographs describe the physical characteristics and
habits of water bugs.

Note to Parents and Teachers

The Insects series supports national science standards on units on
the diversity and unity of life. The series shows that animals have
features that help them live in different environments. This book
describes water bugs and illustrates their parts and habits. The
photographs support early readers in understanding the text. The
repetition of words and phrases helps early readers learn new
words. This book also introduces early readers to subject-specific
vocabulary words, which are defined in the Words to Know section.
Early readers may need assistance to read some words and to use
the Table of Contents, Words to Know, Read More, Internet Sites,
and Index/Word List sections of the book.

Table of Contents

4

Water bugs live
in ponds, lakes,
and streams.

water strider

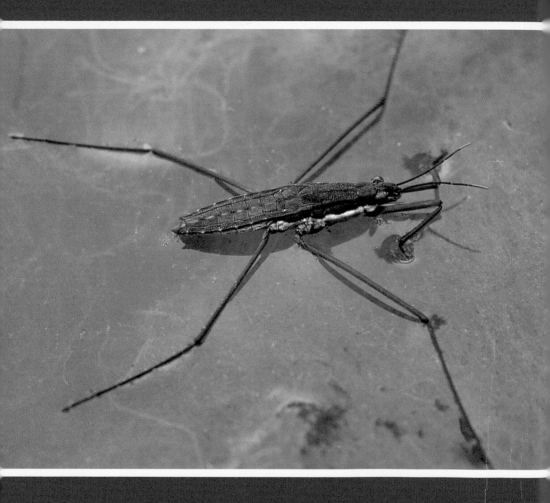

Some water bugs
walk on top of water.

water strider

8

Some water bugs
swim underwater.

giant water bug

Some water bugs
swim upside down.

backswimmer

12

Some water bugs breathe air through a tube. The tube reaches through the water and into the air.

water scorpion

beak

Water bugs can suck
their food through a beak.

giant water bug

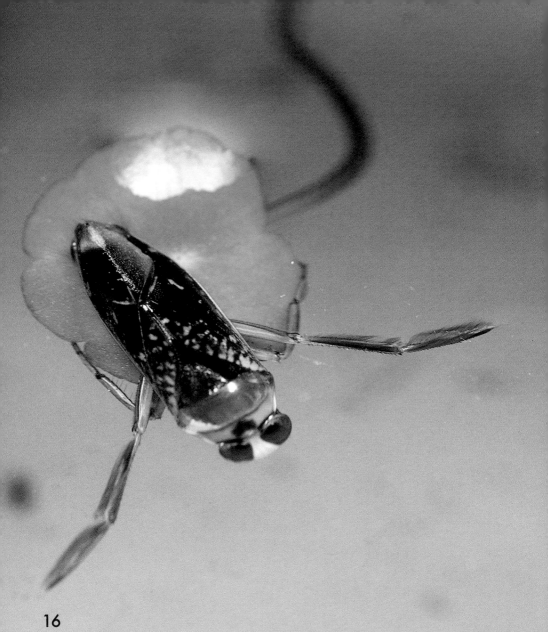

Some water bugs
have legs shaped
like paddles.

backswimmer

claws

Some water bugs
have claws.

giant water bug

Giant water bugs can catch and eat small fish.

giant water bug

Words to Know

beak—the hard part of a water bug's mouth; water bugs can use their beak to suck their food.

breathe—to take in air; some water bugs breathe air through a tube at the end of their abdomen.

bug—a kind of insect that has a beak with sucking mouthparts; water bugs live in or on the water.

claw—a hard, curved nail on the feet of some animals; some water bugs have claws; they use their claws to catch prey.

giant water bug—a very big, flat water bug; giant water bugs can grow to be 2.5 inches (6.3 centimeters) long.

underwater—under the surface of the water; more than 1,000 kinds of water bugs live underwater.

Read More

Miller, Sara Swan. *True Bugs: When Is a Bug Really a Bug?* Animals in Order. New York: Franklin Watts, 1998.

Schaefer, Lola M. *What Is an Insect?* Animal Kingdom. Mankato, Minn.: Pebble Books, 2001.

Wilsdon, Christina. *National Audobon Society First Field Guide: Insects.* New York: Scholastic, 1998.

Internet Sites

Animal Facts—Giant Water Bug
http://www.zoo.org/educate/fact_sheets/waterbug/waterbug.htm

Aquatic Critters: Water Bugs
http://mbgnet.mobot.org/fresh/slide/water.htm

Giant Water Bug
http://www.insects.org/entophiles/hemiptera/hemi_005.html

Pond Bugs
http://www.achilles.net/ofnc/pondbugs.htm

Index/Word List

Word Count: 76
Early-Intervention Level: 5

Editorial Credits
Mari C. Schuh, editor; Timothy Halldin, cover designer; Kia Bielke, production designer; Kimberly Danger, photo researcher

Photo Credits
Connie Toops, 12
David Liebman, 16
Dwight R. Kuhn, 10, 14, 18, 20
James P. Rowan, 8
John S. Reid, 1
L. West/Bruce Coleman Inc., 4
Visuals Unlimited/C & G Merker, cover; Gary Meszaros, 6

24